...God's people were waiting
for God's special plan.
For he'd promised a **King**
filled with power and might
who could banish the bad stuff
and make all things right!

And they'd wondered
for **years**
how God's plan
would unfurl...

"I am the Lord's servant!"

she boldly declared,
for she trusted in God
even though she was scared.

But when Joseph had noticed
that she was expecting,

An angel turned up
to tell Joseph the facts.
This baby was **King!**
And it wasn't just that...

This bump-to-be-born was a **saviour** in skin. King Jesus was coming to save us from sin!

He didn't expect it.
He'd **never** have guessed.
A King who could save us
from all of our mess?!

It was God's Holy Spirit
who'd given this life,
so Joseph obeyed
and made Mary his wife.

They set off to Bethlehem,
as was decreed –
Joseph
and Mary
and baby-to-be.

And when they arrived,
they were desperate to rest.
They'd assumed they'd find room...

but **nothing** was left!

**TRY ROUND
THE BACK!**

So when the time came,
they weren't cosy and warm...

They didn't expect it.
They'd **never** have guessed
that the King would be born
where the animals rest.

But Jesus was humble
enough to live **here.**
He shared in our suffering
and took up our tears.

Now, while crowds in the town
were all deep in their sleep,
there were shepherds nearby,
watching over their sheep.

Until something disrupted
the darkness of night...

The sky seemed to open,
exploding with light!
The glory of God
all around them displayed!
The angel declaring,

Do not be afraid!

"I bring you good news
that will cause you great joy!
The **Saviour** is born as a baby
- a boy!"

Then, in awe and amazement,
they spread the good news.

Now, far in the east,
men most clever and wise
had seen a strange star
that was starting to rise.

They knew that a **King** was the cause of this star, so they set off to find him and followed it far...

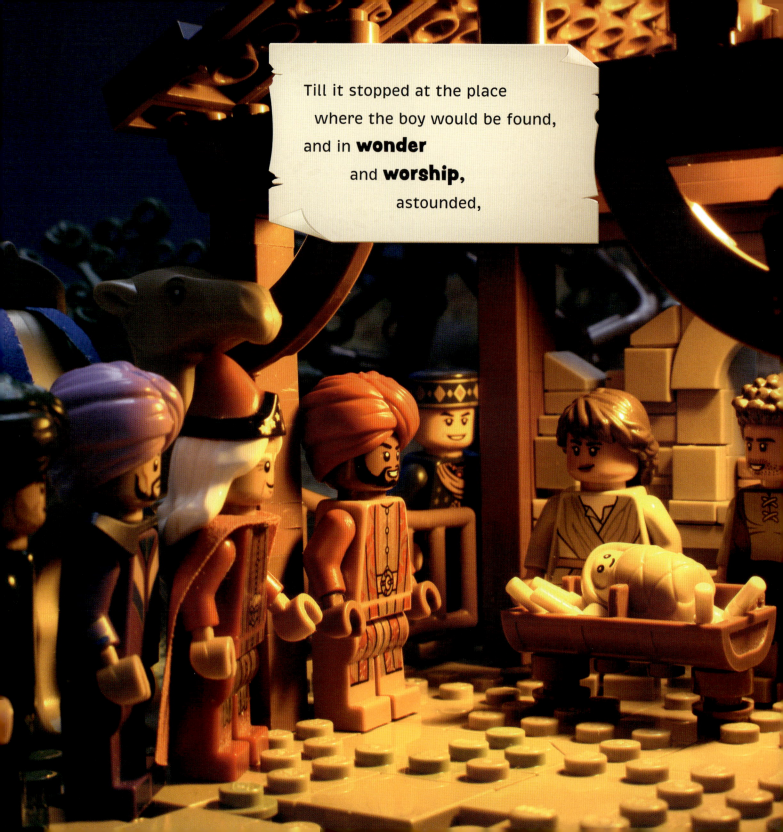

Till it stopped at the place
where the boy would be found,
and in **wonder**
and **worship,**
astounded,

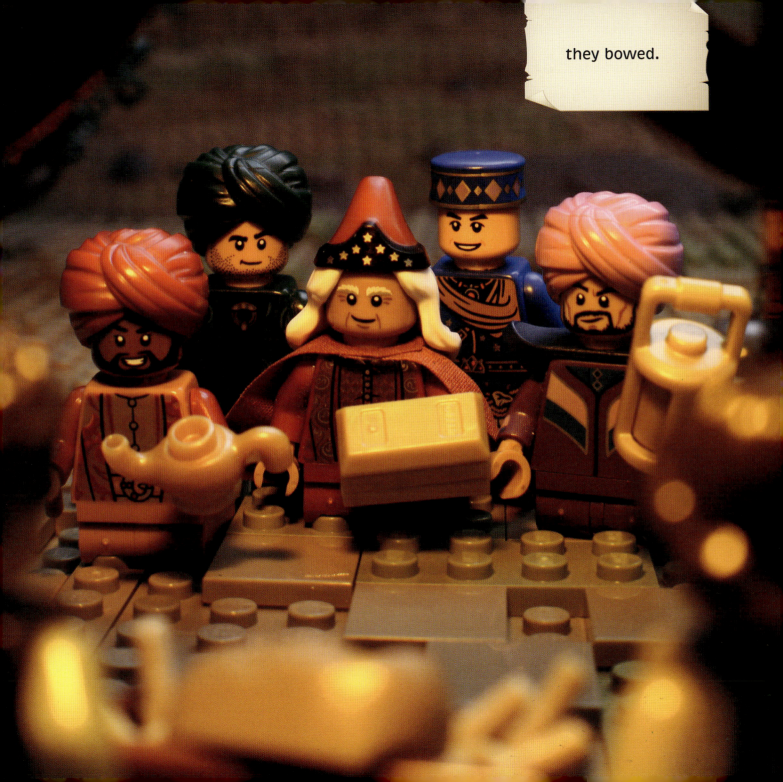

they bowed.

For here was the **King**
filled with power and might
to banish the bad stuff
and make all things right!

Yet this King was **little.**
And this King could cry.
He was fragile and feeble
and one day would die.

We'd **never** have guessed

God would choose to be poor.

But he made himself nothing,

so we could be sure...

— BRICK BY BRICK —

Build Your Own Nativity!

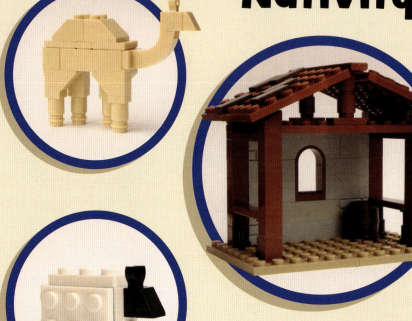

Find instructions for 5 builds and be inspired to create your own stable scene. Just scan the QR code or follow the links!

thegoodbook.co.uk/bricknativity
thegoodbook.com/bricknativity
thegoodbook.com.au/bricknativity